Playa Vista Living

Your Guide to Buying, Selling and Living in Playa Vista, CA

2015
Edition

Tami Humphrey

401 Manhattan Beach Blvd, Suite B
Manhattan Beach, CA 90266
BRE# 01745122

PALM REALTY
BOUTIQUE

Playa Vista Living

Your Guide to Buying, Selling and Living in Playa Vista, CA

By: Tami Humphrey

Contact Tami Humphrey

Phone: (424) 228-8442

Email:
info@PlayaVista-RealEstate.com

Website:
www.PlayaVistaLiving.com

CONTENTS

Acknowledgments   i

1   About the author   Pg 1

2   About Playa Vista   Pg 5

3   Frequently Asked Questions   Pg 25

4   Choosing the right realtor   Pg 35

5   Buying a home   Pg 41

6   Selling your home   Pg 47

7   The homes in Playa Vista   Pg 55

8   Area statistics & demographics   Pg 89

9   Contact Tami Humphrey   Pg 93

ACKNOWLEDGMENTS

It's the residents of Playa Vista, past, present and future
that help me succeed in my business and give me great joy
by allowing me to help them buy or sell their homes.
Thank you for your support and for allowing me to be
your real estate agent and more importantly your friend.

I'd also like to thank Greg Brinson from Maximum
Visibility Marketing in Los Angeles for providing support
and direction and helping to make this book possible.

1.

ABOUT THE AUTHOR

Tami is a Southern California native and has lived everywhere from Thousand Oaks to San Diego, but when she discovered Playa Vista, she finally felt a true connection to a community. She played volleyball for the UC-San Diego team and loves the close proximity to the beach, where she can play her favorite sport in the sun and the sand. Tami enjoys an active lifestyle, whether it's practicing Bikram Yoga, cheering on the Dodgers or enjoying the local good life with friends and family at area restaurants, shops and events.

It's fitting Tami takes such pride in the Playa Vista lifestyle. "Vista" literally means "view" in Spanish, and her perspective has always been what's made her successful in life and business. Her creative point of view and positive outlook are the keys to her success as a leading local real estate professional. Though she works with buyers and sellers throughout the area, her natural focus is on the Playa Vista community she loves so much.

The Perspective You Need

Tami was here for the initial growth, as well as the lean economic years before Playa Vista expanded once again with the addition of Phase 2. In other words, she's been here through it all and knows exactly what makes this community special. Tami has a wealth of knowledge when it comes to different developments and condo complexes, which is valuable information to the home buyers she works with—from varying HOA dues and Mello-Roos fees to special lifestyle amenities provided by each community. In fact, Tami was chosen by HGTV to represent a couple buying a home in Playa Vista on the show "House Hunters," which aired in 2013.

For sellers, Tami knows what it takes to stage and market Playa Vista homes and condos to attract more buyers and get the best return on investment. She's always had a creative eye and detailed approach. Tami helps clients with staging and hires a professional photographer to take pictures of the house for online marketing and custom listing brochures for each property. This approach has earned her the "Five Star Professional" award in Los Angeles Magazine—three years in a row and counting.

The Attention You Deserve

Most importantly, Tami's personal style of service and positive energy make clients feel comfortable with her every step of the way toward a successful home purchase or sale. When you add it all up, you get The Playa Vista Perspective you need and the attention you deserve. Contact Tami Humphrey today and get more out of your next move.

Just take a look at what some of her satisfied clients are saying:

"We could not have been more pleased with our experience. Tami exudes professionalism. She was on top of every aspect of the transaction. We can't recommend Tami enough!"

—Brook & Beth Porter

"Anyone who gets the opportunity to be a client of Tami's should consider themselves blessed. She has been a dream to work with. She has amazing knowledge of Southern California. We remain grateful to have had such a memorable experience."

—Trevor & Bethany Clark

"Tami has been amazing to work with. She's very professional and went above and beyond for me and my family. Thank you for making my dream of becoming a homeowner come true!"

—Paul Khloyian.

"Tami Humphrey sold our condo in Playa Vista in 2013. She was on top of everything and delivered faster than we expected. She's extremely professional, knowledgeable and personable. Our unit sold within days of us listing it! We truly appreciate her level of competency and service provided. She exceeded all our expectations and will definitely use her again and again! Tami is truly a gem! "

- Summer H

"We recently sold our condo using Tami Humphrey as our real estate agent. We are extremely satisfied with the level of service provided by Tami. Being an out of town seller, we had certain concerns but Tami's performance, as our advocate, was outstanding. Not only did she find a buyer within a week, we were about to handle every aspect of the transaction via phone, email, and notary, which was very important to us. The level of communication was fantastic. We found working with her a joy and she was there to help us during every step of the process. Her in-depth knowledge of the industry and market, along with her strong work ethic makes her an excellent real estate agent. We would recommend her to anyone looking to buy or sell property."

- Judy Schulz

"We hired Tami as our buying agent in Playa Vista, we are extremely happy with our experience. If you are looking for property in Playa Vista area, Tami is definitely the expert to go to. I first saw her on HGTV, and then I thought she must mainly focus on higher price properties, and we were looking for 1 bedroom condo, after expressing my interest to her, she was really responsive, and sent me new listing every time as soon as it's available. She was super professional and on top of everything from making offer to closing; she made our first home buying experience so easy and stress-free. If we are going to buy another property in Playa Vista in the future, we will ask Tami again FOR SURE "

- Lu Lu

2.

ABOUT PLAYA VISTA, CA

Playa Vista is a unique community located less than 2-miles from the Pacific Ocean and adjacent to Marina del Rey. The property has a long history which includes being home to a cattle ranch in the 1800s. Perhaps what it's most famous for is its history as an airport which was the vision of Howard Hughes. The hangars are still present towards the east end of the property and it was in these hangars that the famous "Spruce Goose" aircraft was built. The hangars and many of the surrounding buildings have recently been upgraded and modified into some pretty fantastic office and creative spaces, but they retain their look from when they were first erected many decades ago. Big things are happening in this area when it comes to commercial spaces and business endeavors. Whether it's a new start-up or an expanding global corporation, Playa Vista is proving to be an attractive area for a number of industries, including technology and media. Many are referring to the area as "Silicon Valley South" for very good reason.

Construction on the first phase of Playa Vista began around 2002 and Phase two should have begun shortly after phase one was complete. The downturn in the economy brought everything to a screeching halt in 2007 and phase two only began construction in late 2012.

The hangars where Howard Hughes' Spruce Goose was built

The Runway

What current residents are most excited about is having access to even more great restaurants and other retail establishments. The legendary parcel of land that once gave rise to Howard Hughes' aerospace empire is undergoing a transformation into 'Runway,' a large-scale mixed-use center that will offer unique shopping, dining, entertainment and living space in the heart of the Playa Vista community. The development team, led by Lincoln Property Company, Phoenix Property Company and Paragon Commercial Group, has begun construction to this lifestyle center that will soon connect the phase one residential community and the Campus at Playa Vista.

The project will include 221,000 square feet of retail, 420 apartments and 35,000 square feet of office space spread across three separate buildings. Construction is expected to last less than three years, with tenants opening their doors early in 2015.

Several of the nation's top brands have been signing on to be a part of the action at Runway. Upscale grocer Whole Foods will move into a 35,755 square-foot space adjacent to McConnell Avenue, on the retail center's ground level. The grocery store will be a first of its kind in Playa Vista, with well-stocked aisles of organic produce, grass-fed beef, a natural juice bar and a wide assortment of supplements for healthy eating. Down the street, the Cinemark multiplex at Runway will feature nine screens in over 46,000 square feet and the company's NextGen design concept with RealD 3D capability, self-serve concession stands and an open plaza with a cocktail lounge.

Confirmed tenants as of October 2014

- **Whole Foods**   http://www.wholefoodsmarket.com

  Who are we? Well, we seek out the finest natural and organic foods available, maintain the strictest quality standards in the industry, and have an unshakeable commitment to sustainable agriculture. Add to that the excitement and fun we bring to shopping for groceries, and you start to get a sense of what we're all about. Oh yeah, we're a mission-driven company too.

- **Cinemark**   http://bit.ly/1u8BMWj

  Extra large, extreme entertainment! Ceiling–to-floor and wall-to-wall screen, custom sound and premium seating ensure that every seat is an intense sensory experience. Reserve-Level Includes the Following Amenities: Luxury Seating with Tables, Private Balcony Access to Auditoriums, Full Bar and Lounge, Expanded Dining Menu. All-digital new generation of entertainment! With crisp, bright, ultra-realistic 3D images so lifelike you feel like you've stepped inside the movie. All stadium seating, Cafe, Bar.

- **Hopdoddy Burger Bar**   http://www.hopdoddy.com

  Hopdoddy was created to express the perfect union of burgers and beer: Handcrafted Beer (Hop) + (Doddy), the nickname given to the native cow in Aberdeen, Scotland. At Hopdoddy our passion is to bring you the freshest available, all-natural ingredients. Daily in-house we grind hormone/antibiotic free black angus beef, bake our own buns from scratch & cut our own Kennebec Fries

- **800 Degrees**   http://www.800degreespizza.com

Here at 800 Degrees, we strive to honor the heritage of Old World Italian tradition, where the integrity of ingredients is paramount. California grown tomatoes, locally made fresh mozzarella, and handcrafted crust made with flour from the ancient Molino San Felice in Naples, Italy are complemented by only the best charcuterie and local vegetables. While we offer a few favorite combinations, feel free to personalize your pizza with your choice of ingredients. Your pizza will be baked and ready before you even leave the counter! Come in and create your masterpiece.

- **SOL Cocina**   http://www.solcocina.com

SOL was inspired by the best of coastal Baja California, and grew out of many memorable surf trips we've taken down the spectacular peninsula. In a casual, friendly setting, SOL offers an upscale Mexican dining experience that celebrates authentic flavors and Mexican traditions with an ever-changing array of fresh seafood and seasonal fresh ingredients.

- **ROC Kitchen**

- **Urban Plates**   http://www.urbanplates.com

Farm to plate and won't break the bank. Urban Plates is a fresh new concept in dining out.

- **Lyfe Kitchen**   http://www.lyfekitchen.com

Great food can do amazing things. It can make you feel better. It can support local farms. Promote sustainability. Reward environmentally sound businesses. Give back to the community. And, best of all, it will make you savor every single bite. Great tasting food that's also good for you. Is that possible? Good thing we knew just who to call. Chef Art Smith and Chef Jeremy Bringardner. Our executive chefs combined have decades of award-winning expertise. They personally created the amazing menu we have today.

- **Panini Cafe** http://www.mypaninicafe.com

The food at any Café is distinctive and extraordinarily fresh and healthy. We use only the finest quality ingredients, including the best imported olive oil and low-fat cheeses, and all our produce and breads are delivered fresh daily. With a commitment to quality and creativity, we offer incredible variety of foods for breakfast, lunch and dinner. Our Italian Mediterranean influenced kitchen gains inspiration from the best cuisine Europe and the Middle East has to offer.

- **N'iceCream** http://www.ilovenicecream.com

N'iceCream is a young, dynamic and innovative family owned company, specializing in freshly-made organic gelato sorbet and Italian style frozen yogurt.

- **Starbucks** http://www.starbucks.com

To say Starbucks purchases and roasts high-quality whole bean coffees is very true. That's the essence of what we do – but it hardly tells the whole story. Our coffeehouses have become a beacon for coffee lovers everywhere. Why do they insist on Starbucks? Because they know they can count on genuine service, an inviting atmosphere and a superb cup of expertly roasted and richly brewed coffee every time.

- **The Studio MDR** http://www.thestudiomdr.com

The Studio (MDR)™ brings the intensity of fitness guru Sebastien Lagree's pilates-inspired workout to Marina Del Rey, Culver City and Playa Vista. The laid back beach vibe disappears as soon as the music starts pumping and you prepare your body for an intense, muscle quivering, shirt-drenching workout. The Lagree Fitness workout is a total-body program that melds together elements of pilates, cardio training and weight-bearing activity to create a revolutionary, one-of-a-kind exercise program.

Our state of the art Megaformers provide constant resistance and infinitely more exercise options than a traditional reformer; it allows the body to shift quickly and smoothly from one exercise to another to increase heart rate and get the blood pumping. The Megaformer attacks each and every muscle in a very concentrated and focused manner to sculpt strong, powerful and lean bodies in a safe and measured way.

- **18|8 Fine Men's Salon**   http://www.eighteeneight.com

18|8 transforms men to look and perform their best, thanks to our expertise in men's hair care, styling, grooming, products ...and consultation. We provide a truly authentic & innovative experience. A trusted place for men to have a professional grooming experience.

- **Varnish Lab**   http://www.varnishlab.com

Our Philosophy:
Varnish Lab isn't just another nail salon, it's a complete nail spa experience. And we've built that experience around our three core beliefs:

Looking amazing is about feeling amazing:
Taking care of yourself isn't just an indulgence. It's what gives you the confidence to shine in every situation and pampering yourself isn't just a luxury, because it gives you the energy to go from day to evening, day after day. We offer the highest level of service to make these important "me-times" the best they can be, so we can help you stay on top of your game.

You can't reenergize without energy:
Tranquility has its place, but some spa environments are about as exciting as an afternoon nap. We don't want to take you down for the count, so Varnish Lab is designed to perk you up from the moment you step inside. Pops of color, glam touches and your favorite tunes greet you at every turn, creating a positive energy that's maintained by our friendly, expert staff.

Cleanliness is next to heavenliness

We take pride in maintaining immaculate surroundings for our guests, because your health and comfort are our top priorities. From our unique foot bath bowls to our medical-grade sanitization techniques, all of our materials and procedures have been chosen to give you peace of mind, so your visit can be truly relaxing.

- **Chase Bank**   http://www.chase.com

- **Wells Fargo Bank**   http://www.wellsfargo.com

- **CVS Pharmacy**   http://www.cvs.com

Existing Retail

- **Piknic**   http://www.piknicplayavista.com

PIKNIC of Playa Vista offers a rousing simplicity with our menu paired with a modern and versatile ambiance in a location that you would not expect. Join us for lunch and you will soon be choosing one of our crisp salads, carved artisan sandwiches or gourmet hamburgers. The waterfall gently spills over the sounds of lively lunch guests and transitions the changing vibe that comes with every evening. The subtle dimming of the lights overhead stretch towards the new glow of the candles blushing from the tables, as our dinner menu takes its place. Only the best ingredients and products are used in our incredible menu. Start off with our unique

Mediterranean Platter and be faced to choose from Chilean Sea Bass or Delmonico steak and Alaskan Halibut. PIKNIC extends outside of the restaurant as well. Take advantage of our Corporate Catering service for your next luncheon or private event!

*** Just prior to this book going to print, Piknic was sold and is under new ownership. The new name will be GULP and there will be renovations to the restaurant's interior and many changes to the food and drink menus.

- **Sweet Fish Sushi**   http://www.sweetfishsushi.com

Since 2010, Sweet Fish Sushi Bar and Restaurant has been serving up innovative Japanese sushi for lunch and dinner in Playa Vista, California. With hundreds of choices for sushi restaurants, Los Angeles is second only to Tokyo for ingenuity and diversity in Japanese cuisine, and Sweet Fish continually breaks with the convention of traditional sushi restaurants. Both proprietor and chef diligently innovate to ensure the menu is always able to offer patrons a new take on old favorites. Tucked into the serene Pacific Promenade in the new Playa Vista development, Sweet Fish shares nothing with sushi bars along Lincoln Boulevard or crammed in the corner of a Marina Del Rey strip mall. With a primary focus on service and comfort, Sweet Fish is a welcome change from the average sushi restaurant and showcases a sophisticated mastery of Japanese fare from both the kitchen and the sushi bar. Centrally located a short drive from Playa Del Rey and Marina Del Rey, sushi and Japanese cuisine served in a comfortable and stylish setting are always close at hand.

- **Yoga Vista**   http://www.yogavistastudio.com

- **Hollyway Cleaners** http://www.hollywaycleaners.com

At Hollyway Cleaners, we are committed to providing our clients with the highest quality environmentally friendly garment care by the most experienced and friendly team in the industry. Our focus is to become a leader in our chosen market by providing new and innovative services and products that exceed our customer's expectations. We will continuously improve all of our processes in order to increase satisfaction, quality and value for our customers. Our success is a direct result of our re-investing in our organization, our employees, and most importantly in the community we serve. Our neighbors are our customers.

- **Bank of America**   http://www.bankofamerica.com

- **The Coffee Bean**   http://www.coffeebean.com

Born and brewed in Southern California since 1963, The Coffee Bean & Tea Leaf is the oldest and largest privately held specialty coffee and tea retailer in the United States.

- **Yummy.com**   http://www.yummy.com

Yummy.com is your online grocer! Our mission is to delight you with a superior online grocery experience that is faster and more convenient than a trip to the store. Since our founding in 2002, we have worked hard to perfect our proprietary order management system that allows us to fulfill our online order in as little as 30 minutes.

- **Pinkberry**   http://www.pinkberry.com

Pinkberry launched in Los Angeles, California in 2005 as the original brand that reinvented the category and now has more than 250 stores worldwide in 20 countries. Today, Pinkberry continues to delight everyone we serve with an experience made up of distinctive product, outstanding service and inspirational design. Pinkberry creates one of a kind, light and refreshing treats with an uncompromising commitment to quality. Pinkberry continues to lead the frozen yogurt category in international expansion.

- **McClintock Dental** http://www.mcclintockdental.com

Dr. Robert A. (Sandy) McClintock has practiced dentistry in the LAX-Marina del Rey area of Southern California since graduating from the University of Southern California (USC) School of Dentistry. He subsequently served on the USC faculty as an associate professor of operative and team dentistry. He is a lecturer in the field of cosmetic and restorative dentistry.

Dr. McClintock is active in numerous dental organizations including the American Dental Association, California Dental Association, The Western Dental Society and the Newport Harbor Academy of Dentistry.

- **Playa Pilates**   http://www.playapilates.com

Since 2004 Playa Pilates has been the premier provider of individual and group instruction across Los Angeles. The modern boutique style studio specializes in programs personalized for individual fitness goals or needs. The Pilates equipment uses spring tension to both strengthen and support the body while it learns to move more efficiently. This technique creates a body that looks natural and feels fit. Playa Pilates will continually challenge you to focus on strengthening your core all the while conditioning your mind and body to work together, creating a well rounded workout for your entire body.

With the calm and inviting atmosphere, Playa Pilates offers a studio space that feels like an extension of your home. Our instructors strive to be the best and continue their education yearly. We stick with teaching pure Pilates (no hybrids or made up exercises here!) to local communities for all those who seek wellness, relief from injury, and wholeness of mind and body. You won't find a more relaxing environment or better method of exercise to improve your way of life. We hope to see you soon!

- **Playa Vista Medical**   http://www.pvmedcenter.com

Playa Vista Urgent Care is a walk-in clinic, providing convenient medical services without an appointment, for the Playa Vista, Marina del Rey, Playa del Rey, Westchester, Venice, Santa Monica,

Culver City, and Del Rey areas. We provide you and your family with the foremost advanced urgent care compared to other clinics.

- **Slice Pizza**   http://www.theslicepv.com

Located in the beautiful Fountain Park building in Playa Vista. At The Slice, we take pride in every hand-tossed pizza and dish we create. By utilizing local farm fresh ingredients with our New York inspired recipes, The Slice offers a pizza like no other.

The Social and Recreational Clubs

The CenterPointe Club

The CenterPointe Club, a 26,000 sq. ft. recreation and activity center, which includes 2 pools, a spa, fitness center, business center, meeting room and indoor and outdoor event spaces. There are also acres of preserved passive and active open space.

The Resort (Opening Spring 2015)

The Resort is planned to be completed in the Spring of 2015 and the opening will be announced as construction comes to a close. This is our newest resident activity club with resort-style amenities including a new two-level, state-of-the-art fitness center with indoor/outdoor spaces and a cool pool deck with an outdoor fireplace, cabanas, junior Olympic pool, adult pool and spa and kids' pool and spa. Plus, the catering kitchen and chef-inspired demonstration kitchen will be the perfect backdrop for many gourmet parties and events.

One of several pools at The Resort

Sports and Recreation

As part of the monthly homeowners fees, residents have access to several athletic amenities. These include a baseball diamond, tennis courts, basketball courts, walking trails, a soccer field, playgrounds, putting greens and for our furry friends there are several dog parks. With Playa Vista being located just 2-miles from the beach, access to miles of bike and running paths is almost outside your front door.

The Campus - Business Park

The appeal of Playa Vista and the surrounding areas to both start-ups and well-established companies is immense. This section of Los Angeles has plenty of newly built or renovated commercial space all within a short distance to cafes, shops, parks, and the beach. Employees can surf before work, eat lunch at any one of a number of fantastic restaurants, or easily make it to a happy hour on their way home from the office.

Google recently purchased 12 acres in Playa Vista for a whopping $120 million. Some are saying that this move by Google shows that Playa Vista is becoming the tech and innovation capital of Los Angeles. Approximately

6,000 jobs could be brought to the area by this project alone depending on the direction Google takes when developing the land.

This area is close to a major airport (LAX) and major freeways, making it as accessible and convenient as it is beautiful and inviting.

Current Business Tenants:

- **YouTube Space**

  The flagship location for YouTube Space is designed especially for creators to produce video content, learn new skills, and collaborate with the YouTube creative community.

YouTube Space facility in Playa Vista

- **Belkin**

  For nearly 30 years it has been our passion and our mission to create products that make people's lives better, easier and more fulfilling. From wireless home networking and entertainment, to mobile accessories, energy management, and an extensive range of cables, Belkin products enhance the technology that connects us to the people, activities and experiences we love...

- **Facebook**

Founded in 2004, Facebook's mission is to give people the power to share and make the world more open and connected. People use Facebook to stay connected with friends and family, to discover what's going on in the world, and to share and express what matters to them.

- **California Pizza Kitchen**

Almost immediately after the first location opened, we expanded from California to more than 250 locations in more than 30 states and 11 countries. But it doesn't stop there; you'll also find us bringing smiles to the pizza aisle in your grocer's freezer, taking the edge off travel fatigue in major airports all over the world, feeding eager fans at sports stadiums and students on college campuses.

- **Supra Studio**

- **FoxSports.com**

- **ICANN**

ICANN is a not-for-profit public-benefit corporation with participants from all over the world dedicated to keeping the Internet secure, stable and interoperable. It promotes competition and develops policy on the Internet's unique identifiers. Through its coordination role of the Internet's naming system, it does have an important impact on the expansion and evolution of the Internet.

- **Fox Interactive Media**

Fox Interactive Media is a network of companies in the industry of media; news, education, and information services.

- **Konami**

Konami Digital Entertainment, Inc. (KDEI), a wholly owned subsidiary of Konami Corporation (NYSE: KNM), is a leading, global developer, publisher and manufacturer of electronic entertainment properties, specializing in the home video game market.

- **USC Institute for Creative Technologies**

At the University of Southern California Institute for Creative Technologies (ICT) leaders in artificial intelligence, graphics, virtual reality and narrative advance low-cost immersive techniques and technologies to solve problems facing service members, students and society.

- **Rubicon Project**

Rubicon Project is a leading technology company automating the buying and selling of advertising. Relentless in its efforts for innovation, Rubicon Project has engineered one of the largest real-time cloud and Big Data computing systems, processing trillions of transactions within milliseconds each month.

The company's pioneering technology created a new model for the advertising industry – similar to what NASDAQ did for stock trading. Rubicon Project's automated advertising platform is used by the world's leading publishers and applications to transact with top brands around the globe.

- **Gehry Technologies**

Gehry Technologies is an AEC technology company providing leading edge solutions to the industry's most challenging projects.

Our clients include some of the most recognized international architects, engineers, contractors, and owners working across the globe.

We offer a different approach to AEC. We leverage some of the world's leading technologies with world class implementation team to solve our clients' unique professional ambitions. Our team includes architects, engineers, builders, computer scientist and management consultants.

We support the adoption of BIM technology and processes through project based services, allowing teams to advance their use of these critical systems while meeting project schedules. We provide training and knowledge transfer as part of every engagement. Working with Gehry Technologies, project teams can innovate with confidence, while serving shared goals of highest quality, speed, and maximum value.

- **72 and Sunny**

72andSunny creates cultural impact on behalf of brands. The company was named "Agency of the Year" for the past two years by Ad Age and Adweek. With offices in Los Angeles, New York and Amsterdam, 72andSunny services clients including Activision, American Legacy Foundation / truth, Carl's Jr./Hardee's, ESPN, Google, Samsung, Smirnoff, Sonos, Starbucks, Tillamook and Target.

- **Rovi**

Rovi is leading the way to a more personalized entertainment experience. Our pioneering guides, data, and recommendations continue to drive program search and navigation on millions of devices on a global basis. With a new generation of cloud-based discovery capabilities and emerging solutions for interactive advertising and audience analytics, Rovi is enabling premier brands worldwide to increase their reach, drive consumer satisfaction and create a better entertainment experience across multiple screens. Rovi holds over 5,000 issued or pending patents worldwide and is headquartered in Santa Clara, California.

- **Cybercoders**

CyberCoders is a subsidiary of On Assignment, a leading global provider of in-demand, skilled professional across all industries.

Founded in 1999 by Lance Miller, CyberCoders' mission is to improve lives by matching great people with great companies. Here at CyberCoders, we believe in the passionate pursuit of the right candidate for the right job. We recruit professionals for all types of jobs including engineering, technology, sales, executive, financial, accounting, scientific, legal and operational positions across all industries.

- **Brighter**

In business as in nature, what separates the winners from the losers is the ability to adapt to changing conditions. Whether it's responding to increased competition, changing user behaviors or utilizing emerging technology, organizations must be able to adjust their tactics, operations and messages to stay abreast of the marketplace. That's where we come in.

We are an adaptive agency that designs intelligent strategies that align with the needs of today and adapt to the needs of tomorrow. Our collaborative, user-centered approach carefully considers the realities of your organization and industry in order to deliver practical and sustainable solutions that transform the way you connect with your audience.

- **Los Angeles Clippers Training Center**

The Clippers' $50 million, two-story building in West Los Angeles' Playa Vista neighborhood opened in September, 2008 containing all the bells and whistles associated with a modern NBA training complex, including a duplicate of the Robbins Sports Surfaces wood floor that the team plays on at Staples Center.

21

- **Brookfield Residential**

  Brookfield Residential Properties Inc. is a leading North American land developer and homebuilder with operations in eleven major markets. They entitle and develop land to create master-planned communities and build and sell lots to third-party builders, as well as to their own homebuilding division. They also participate in selected, strategic real estate opportunities, including infill projects, mixed-use developments, infrastructure projects, and joint ventures.

Area Attractions and Shopping

- Los Angeles International Airport (3 miles)
- Closest Beach, Playa del Rey (2 miles)
- Fox Hills Mall (2 miles)
- Sony Pictures Studio Tour (4.9 miles)
- 3rd Street Promenade (6 miles)
- Santa Monica Pier (5.5 miles)
- Manhattan Beach (7.5 miles)
- Hermosa Beach (9.7 miles)
- Redondo Beach (10 miles)
- Century City Mall (9 miles)
- Rodeo Drive (9.5 miles)
- Universal Studios (15 miles)
- Downtown Los Angeles (16 miles)
- Staples Center (16 miles)
- Dodger's Stadium (18 miles)
- Disneyland (37 miles)
- Warner Brothers Studio Tour (16.2 miles)
- Knott's Berry Farm (33 miles)
- Six Flags (37.6 miles)
- Hollywood Walk of Fame (12 miles)

- Santa Barbara (90 miles)
- Palm Springs (124 miles)
- San Diego (127 miles)
- San Francisco (384 miles)

Free Playa Vista Shuttle Services

The Playa Vista Beach Shuttle in action throughout the summer! The community shuttle takes you to and from your favorite destinations on the Westside every Friday through Sunday. Hop on the shuttle to avoid looking for parking or fighting through traffic and get to where you want to go with ease. Spend an afternoon by the Marina or shop to your heart's content along Abbott Kinney Boulevard. Plus, you will be able to **track its location on NextBus.com**, so you spend less time waiting.

The beach shuttle service also connects riders to the Marina del Rey WaterBus, which provides ferry service throughout the Marina.

The Campus Shuttle runs Mondays through Fridays from 11am to 3pm and offers various stops throughout our community.

Shuttle Stops:
Campus Center Drive and Bluff Creek Drive
Bluff Creek Drive and Artisans Way
Waterfront Drive and Lake Center Drive
IMAX HQ
McConnell Avenue and Runway Road
Para Way/Concerto Lofts
Seabluff Drive/Pinkberry

Tami Humphrey

3.

FREQUENTLY ASKED QUESTIONS

What is Mello Roos?

Along with your Los Angeles County property tax (approximately 1.2%), Playa Vista home owners also pay a Mello Roos tax. In order to develop our community the City and the developers, with 2/3rds approval of voters, issued bonds under the Mello Roos act of 1982. This bond issuance paid for our infrastructure such as sewers, parks, traffic improvements, utilities and a fire station.

How much is it and how long will it last?

Mello-Roos bonds are paid for as a special tax on your property that will be levied for 40 years from the date of possession of the home's first owner. The annual tax is derived from a somewhat complicated calculation but the following chart will give you an idea of what you will pay according the square footage of your home. *The exact amount can vary slightly as the tax can increase by up to 2% per year.*

Playa Vista Phase II homes do not have a Mello Roos tax. The cost of developing this part of the community's infrastructure was paid off

by the builders and the expense is reflected in the selling price of the new homes.

Playa Vista Mello Roos Chart 2014-2015

Description	Designation (Sq Ft.)	FY 2014-2015 Assigned Maximum Special Tax per unit	FY 2014-2015 Actual Special Tax per unit
Single Family Home	>3,800	$ 12,495.06	$ 8,499.14
Single Family Home	>3,500-3,800	$ 11,999.76	$ 8,162.24
Single Family Home	>3,000-3,500	$ 10,741.39	$ 7,306.29
Single Family Home	>2,800-3,000	$ 10,442.41	$ 7,102.93
Single Family Home	>2,550-2,800	$ 7,032.17	$ 4,783.28
Single Family Home	>2,300-2,550	$ 6,329.63	$ 4,305.41
Single Family Home	>2,150-2,300	$ 5,624.38	$ 3,825.70
Single Family Home	>1,850-2,150	$ 5,308.10	$ 3,610.57
Single Family Home	>1,650-1,850	$ 4,220.66	$ 2,870.89
Single Family Home	>1,450-1,650	$ 3,816.87	$ 2,596.23
Single Family Home	>1,200-1,450	$ 3,512.71	$ 2,389.35
Single Family Home	>1,000-1,200	$ 2,639.25	$ 1,795.22
Single Family Home	>825-1,000	$ 2,300.10	$ 1,564.53
Single Family Home	>725-825	$ 2,118.38	$ 1,440.92
Single Family Home	<725	$ 1,940.75	$ 1,320.10
Apartment Property	N/A	$ 3,367.36	$ 2,290.48
Affordable Housing, For Sale	N/A	$ 1,320.31	$ 898.07
Affordable Housing, Rental	N/A	$ 672.93	$ 457.73
Industrial/Office/ Retail	N/A	$2.2476/sq ft	$1.52873/sq ft

HOAs - Playa Vista and Building

Playa Vista Parks and Landscape (PVPAL) HOA

The PVPAL HOA, also known as the master HOA, is currently $230 per month (subject to change) which is paid by all home owners in Playa Vista Phase I and Phase II.

The PVPAL HOA includes:

- Basic cable with one standard box
- High-speed Internet
- Alarm service
- Gym Access at both the Centre Point Club and The Resort
- Pool Access at both the Centre Point Club and The Resort
- The use of all parks, fields and courts
- 24-hour community security personnel

Individual Building and Detached Homes HOA's

Each building's HOA is different and the prices range from $150 to $800 per month in Phase I and from $75 to $900 in Phase II. The variance in price depends on the amenities offered by the building and the number of units in which to divide the cost. Some of the higher priced HOA's are the result of more elevators, less units in the building, a pool or even a concierge.

Here's what's typically included:

- Landscaping in and around the building
- Trash and recycling removal
- Water
- Reserves for maintenance of the common areas
- Management Company Fees
- Fire and Liability Insurance for common areas

- All expenses related to operating entry systems, elevators, lighting and security monitoring

Playa Vista Community Enhancement Fee (who pays: the buyer or the seller?)

What is it and what does it cover?

When a home is sold in Playa Vista 0.75% of the purchase price is paid to Playa Vista Community Services (PVCS). These funds are used for the common good of Playa Vista. The summer shuttles, concerts in the park, outdoor movie nights and seasonal events are a few examples. Plus, a portion is also used for the conservation and protection of the Ballona Wetlands.

Who Pays?

Depending on the current market conditions in Playa Vista either the seller, buyer or a combination of the two will pay this fee. Typically, the seller has paid the Community Enhancement fee, but in a seller's market, a savvy Playa Vista Realtor will explain to their buyers that offering to pay half or all of this line item can be the deciding factor in getting an offer chosen. On the flip side, when representing the seller, your listing agent should be encouraging the buyers' agents to include the community enhancement fee as a part of their client's offer. Keep in mind, as the market changes so should your strategy for negotiating the community enhancement fee.

Property taxes

2014/2015 Tax Rates

Taxing Agency	Tax Year Rate
City- Los Angeles	0.028096
Community College	0.040174
County	0.0
General	1.0
Metro Water Dist	0.0035

Unified Schools   0.146881

Total Year Tax Rate: 1.218651

Are there apartment buildings in the community?

Living on LA's west side isn't cheap whether you're buying or renting. Within Playa Vista there are several apartment buildings where rent can range from the low 2,000s to the high 4,000's or more. As in any neighborhood, there are also condominiums that can be found for rent that are within the various community buildings. If you're considering one of these types of properties, you have to act fast since they get snapped up in a hurry.

Should I be concerned about methane gas?

Methane gas is naturally occurring in Playa Vista, but steps were taken during the construction of the subdivision to mitigate risk. These steps included the installation of a rubber-like barrier, rooftop vents and methane detectors that are located throughout buildings within the community.

Other previously developed areas of Los Angeles also sit atop these naturally occurring deposits but the risk mitigation steps were not taken when those buildings were erected. It was not known to be an issue or concern at the time. Much like newer buildings are built to withstand earthquakes, Playa Vista is safer than any other are in the city when it comes to methane gas.

What type of community events are there?

Part of your community HOA fees goes towards a variety of events throughout the year. When hundreds of residents of Playa Vista convene at Concert Park or The Band Shell for movies or concerts it provides a small town feel right in the heart of Los Angeles. You can visit www.blog.playavista.com for more details as well. Here's a partial list of what you can experience while living here.

- **Movies in the park**

  Throughout the summer on Friday nights from mid June to mid August you can bring your lawn chairs and snacks and enjoy a variety of Hollywood movies. Gourmet food trucks have also become a standard part of the evening with at least half a dozen of them surrounding the park to satisfy your food cravings. In 2014 there were a total of 6 movie nights that included such hits as Frozen, American Hustle, Despicable Me 2 and others.

- **Concerts in the park**

  On a similar schedule as the movies in the park, residents are treated to 6 concerts on Sunday evenings each summer. Gourmet food trucks arrive well before the event so arrive early to beat the lines and to meet your neighbors.

- **Farmers market**

  Visit the farmers market website at www.playavistafm.com. The market sets up every Saturday throughout the year from 9am to 2pm, and from May to September there's also Wednesday nights to look forward to from 4pm to 8pm. You'll find fresh California fruits and vegetables as well as fresh cut flowers, prepared foods and various vendors selling ready to eat items like soups, crepes, pizza, sliders and much, much more.

- **Community yard sales**

  A couple times each year, the community puts on a yard sale in Concert Park. You can reserve a spot and purge some of those items that you no longer use or that no longer fit from all the exercise you get from living the California lifestyle. At the end of the day, you can lug the stuff that didn't sell back home or donate it to the folks at Goodwill that arrive in a truck to make your job easier.

Along with the events I've gone through here, there are also Bagel & Brew days (that's coffee not beer) where you can start off your Saturday with fresh bagels and coffee along with your neighbors. There's a Harvest Fest in the fall with pumpkin carving, food trucks, costume contests and face painting. In early December, rumor has it that Santa Claus has been known to show up for pictures with the children.

Did I mention the beach shuttle? If you love the beach but hate to find parking and deal with the crowds, Playa Vista provides a shuttle service during the summer that will take you to Venice beach. Along the way, there are stops at Fisherman's Village and throughout Marina del Rey. So grab your gear and hitch a ride from any of the bus stops inside the subdivision.

What's the population of Playa Vista?

The first phase's population is approximately 6,500 residents. With the addition of new housing in phase two it will rise to around 12,000.

How many homes are in the community?

Playa Vista's first phase has nearly 3,100 homes and apartments combined. Once Phase II is complete it will add an additional 1,900 apartments and approximately 600 homes and condos along with 200 independent/assisted living homes.

What schools are in the area?

Local public schools in the Los Angeles Unified School District serving

Playa Vista include:

School Name	Rating
Playa Vista Elementary School	No Rating (New)
Orville Wright Engineering and Design Magnet School (Middle School)	3
Marina Del Rey Middle School	3
Westchester Enriched Sciences Magnets (High School)	5
Venice Senior High	6

* Source: www.greatschools.org

The public, charter and private schools serving the Playa Vista area are subject to change.. Los Angeles Unified School District's website, www.lausd.net, and www.greatschool.org are good online resources.

What's the parking situation for residents and visitors?

Depending on the size of condominium or home, each comes with one or more parking spaces that are deeded to the units. Some include a tandem space (vehicles parking one behind the other) and some are side by side. Condominium buildings have guest parking in the garages and there's street parking throughout the community. Streets do have restricted parking on varying days each week during a 2-hour period when you cannot park there and you're guaranteed to get an expensive ticket if you do. Pay attention to the signs and remember to remind your guests to move their vehicle if necessary.

Playa Vista is close to the airport. What about the noise?

Playa Vista is in fact very close to the Los Angeles International Airport, about 3-miles to be exact. Having lived here for 9-years, I can assure you that the airplanes are not a noise issue. Why not check it out for yourself by spending an afternoon enjoying the community while dining out on one of the local restaurant's patios, or enjoying a picnic in the park? You'll get a firsthand experience and see that we get the benefit of being just minutes from an International airport, but we don't have to put up with any of the noise.

Playa Vista's Soccer Field

Tami Humphrey

4.

CHOOSING THE RIGHT AGENT

Choosing the right realtor whether you're buying or selling a house is of paramount importance and can either make you or save you thousands of dollars while helping you avoid unforeseen pitfalls. A home is most likely the single biggest investment you'll ever make, yet many people will take the first realtor that comes along or the relative of a friend that just got into the business without completing the necessary due diligence. You may be thinking that it doesn't make a big difference, but a knowledgeable agent can help your offer get accepted when others can't, or they leverage little known strategies that someone unfamiliar with the area or community you're buying or selling in doesn't know about.

Conduct some investigative research on a short list of agents in order to better gauge their knowledge and experience. Visit their website to ensure that it's professional in appearance and contains good, valuable content. If they have links to social sites, check each of those out. These may not be the deciding factor, but it might reveal the degree to which each one invests time and money in their own business and may be an indicator as to how effectively they operate as a real estate agent and in helping you buy or sell a home.

Below I've outlined some qualifying questions you may want to ask or determine in some way before ever signing a contract. Some are straight forward and you may understand the reason for asking while others you may not have thought of.

For Home Sellers

- How familiar with the area is the real estate agent?

  As is the case in Playa Vista, there's a lot that's unique to the community and an agent from some other area of Los Angeles may not be aware of. This can cost you money or result in mispricing your home.

- Do they live in the area where you're selling?

  This may not be of utmost importance, but if you're trying to decide between two people, it might be one thing that causes you to pick one over the other.

- How long have they lived in the area?

  The longer the better. This is another one that may not carry significant weight when comparing agents, but it would be good to know if someone has lived in the area for years or just moved from out of state.

- How does the agent market your home?

  Get specifics on what the campaign will involve. Does the agent have a list of potential buyers or people that have expressed an interest in the area or will they just post your home to the MLS and wait for an offer to come in?

- Will there be an open house for your property?

   Why or why not? When will it be and how many will be held. There may be reasons to have them and there may be reasons not to, but ask the agent and have them explain their reasoning.

- How many transactions does your agent close each year?

   You don't necessarily need to know the exact number, but knowing that they've had less than 5 might not be the sign of a top, experienced, full-time agent.

- Are they a part-time or full-time agent?

   This is pretty straight forward. You probably want an agent that will be available on a Tuesday at 2:00 and not in a meeting at their other job. If they are, they may be unable to respond to a newly submitted offer or to answer your questions until after 5:00.

- Have the agent explain why you should choose them over another agent and what makes them better.

   Just ask the question and let them answer. Hopefully they have an answer and can tell you what sets them apart.

- Can they help with staging your home and preparing it for sale?

   Some agents will have taken courses on staging themselves or they'll employ a staging company to help in the process. Your agent should be able to give you some tips and pointers on what to do to make your home more saleable.

- Can you provide references of recent clients you've sold homes for?

    Request a couple references of recent clients your potential agent has worked with and ask for permission to contact those people. You may not even choose to contact them, but knowing the agent can provide the names of happy clients says a lot.

- Who will take photos of my home and how many will be posted?

    Like staging, your agent may be a fantastic photographer with all of the proper equipment and the right eye for the job. However, if your agent is going to use their smart phone and is planning on using odd Instagram filters and stretching the images to make the rooms look bigger, you might want to keep looking. As for the quantity, there's a middle ground. You've probably seen listing with too few and some with far too many. Have a look at the agent's current listings to check their quality of work.

For Home Buyers

- How familiar with the area is the real estate agent?

    As is the case in Playa Vista, there's a lot that's unique to the community and an agent from some other area of Los Angeles may not be aware of. This can cost you money by overpaying for a property or result in surprises when you find out about something a local agent would have told you about early in the buying process. Several of those are covered in this book like the HOA fees in the community.

- Do they live in the area where you're buying?

This may not be of utmost importance, but if you're trying to decide between two people, it might be one thing that causes you to pick one over the other.

- How long have they lived in the area?

    The longer the better. This is another one that may not carry significant weight when comparing agents, but it would be good to know if someone has lived in the area for years or just moved from out of state.

- How many transactions does your agent close each year?

    You don't necessarily need to know the exact number, but knowing that they've had less than 5 might not be the sign of a top, experienced agent.

- Are they a part-time or full-time agent?

    This is pretty straight forward. You want an agent that will be available at a moment's notice if you want to make an offer and one that's constantly on the lookout for new listings so you can be one of the first to see it and make an offer if it's the one!

- Have the agent explain why you should choose them over another agent and what makes them better.

    Just ask the question and let them answer. Hopefully they have an answer and can tell you what sets them apart.

- Can you provide references of recent clients you've assisted in the buying process?

    Request a couple references of recent client your potential agent has worked with and ask for permission to contact those people. You may not even choose to contact them, but knowing the agent can provide the names of happy clients says a lot.

5.

BUYING A HOME

Buying a house is generally the biggest investment that the average person will make in his or her life. Following are some important things to consider when purchasing a home.

Should I buy a home?
In addition to providing you with a place to live, owning a home can provide you with a possible investment for many reasons including potential equity growth, the stability that comes with having ownership in a community, and possible tax advantages.

Renting might make more sense for a mobile lifestyle or if you may need to move because of a job change or other factors. If you do not foresee staying in your home for several years, the amount of equity that you build up over the first year or two may be lost through selling costs and real estate commissions.

Can I afford to buy a home?

Normally, you need to have enough savings to cover a down payment of 5% to 20% of the purchase price plus an additional 3% to 7% of this price for closing costs. If you do not have the down payment, you may be able to qualify for a loan under various government programs that are available. *Some buildings in Playa Vista are in litigation with their builder. Obtaining a loan for a unit in one of these buildings may require a larger down payment.*

Before you begin looking for a home decide what you want and can afford. Various factors are considered when a lender qualifies a purchaser for a home purchase including credit history, job stability and the size of the down payment. Prior to shopping for a home you may wish to visit a respected lender to determine the loan you can afford. See mortgage market and loan process.

Selecting an agent

Before you select an agent, do your homework. Interview several real estate agents to determine their level of experience in the area you wish to purchase. Check to ensure that the agent is properly licensed by the California Bureau of Real Estate (CalBRE). Review any disciplinary actions that may be reflected on the licensee record and assess whether or not that information is important to you in your selection of an agent. *Also, ask the agents for the names of past clients and check their references.*

Finding your home

Before you look for a home, you should determine the features that you need such as the location, number of bedrooms, size of the lot and proximity to stores, schools, hospitals, work and other services such as fire and police protection. You should also determine if there are any special taxes, assessments or homeowners association dues that could affect your monthly expenses. *Playa Vista has a community HOA, individual condominium building HOA, and a Mello Roos tax that should be factored into your affordability equation.*

Inspecting the home

Once you find a house that meets your specific needs, you should check the electrical, plumbing and structural integrity of the property. Consider hiring a qualified inspector to evaluate the structural aspects of the home you are considering purchasing. By doing this, you are giving yourself the opportunity to negotiate any necessary repairs with the seller. Under any circumstances, buying a home requires maintenance and sometimes unexpected expenses for repairs. When you make a decision to buy a home, remember to include this in your budget.

Presenting an offer

Decide what you wish to pay for the property. A good basis for this is to determine what other properties in the neighborhood have sold for. Your real estate agent can be a valuable source for this information.

Make sure that your offer contains any contingencies or special conditions that you desire in the contract. This would include your need to qualify for a loan, repairs that you want the seller to complete prior to the close of escrow, as well as pest control inspections, home inspections, home warranty programs, and any other specific items. Remember, if your offer is accepted and thus becomes a binding contract, failure to complete the purchase could affect the return of your deposit.

You should thoroughly review the contract before signing it and make certain that you understand it. If there are portions of the document that you do not understand, you should seek appropriate professional advice. If your real estate agent is unable to adequately answer your questions, you should ask to speak with his or her broker or seek legal advice. Make sure that the offer you sign does not contain any blank spaces that can be filled in after you signed it. Also, avoid giving cash as a deposit or down payment. Instead, always use a check, money order or cashier's check. This provides a permanent record of the money that you have deposited. See purchase contract and receipt for deposit for more information.

Disclosures

There are a number of disclosures that you are entitled to receive during the course of your purchase. Two of the most important disclosures that you should receive in a residential purchase are as follows:

Real Estate Transfer Disclosure Statement (TDS) - This disclosure is completed by the seller and covers the physical condition of the property and potential hazards or defects that may be associated with it. While the seller is principally responsible for the disclosures presented in this document, the agent is also responsible for conducting a visual inspection of the property and disclosing any readily observable defects detected in the process. This document also discloses any special taxes, assessments and other factors that may have a material effect on the value or desirability of the property.

Agency Relationship Disclosure - Your real estate agent is required to provide you with a written disclosure stating whom he or she represents in the transaction. The agent may represent you as the buyer exclusively, or the seller exclusively, or be a dual agent representing both you and the seller. You should carefully review and understand this disclosure as it has a material effect on the level of responsibilities that your agent owes to you.

Depending on the location, age and other factors involved with the residential property that you are purchasing, additional disclosures may be required.

Financing Disclosures - Various financing disclosures are also required in real estate transactions providing you with important details of your loan. In this regard, the two major disclosures required are the Truth in Lending Statement (Regulation Z) and the Real Estate Settlement Procedures Act (RESPA). The Truth in Lending Statement will provide you with important details on the terms and conditions of credit including the amount financed, the finance charge, as well as the annual percentage rate. RESPA requires detailed broker and lender good faith estimates regarding settlement and closing costs to be provided within three days after you apply for a loan. RESPA also requires a HUD Uniform Settlement Statement that provides you with a detailed accounting of actual disbursements and closing costs upon the completion of your loan transaction. Learn about real estate financing Denotes a PDF document options and required disclosures before entering into any purchase contract.

Public Report - In all common interest facilities which have homeowners association dues, as well as in the initial offering of homes in standard subdivisions located outside city limits, a public report issued by the CalBRE is required. The public report is a detailed statement, which discloses to prospective buyers pertinent facts about the subdivision. The report includes information about utilities, water, roads, soil, geologic conditions, title, zoning, use restrictions, hazards, and the financial arrangements that have been made for the completion of the subdivision.

Escrow and title

You have a right to negotiate with the seller if you have a preference as to the escrow and title company that will be used in your transaction. The Escrow Company is a neutral third party with the responsibility of protecting the interests of both the buyer and seller. The escrow officer ensures that all terms of the contract as detailed in the escrow instructions have been met and that the appropriate deeds are recorded upon the close of the transaction. The Title Company provides an insurance policy to protect the buyer and the lender against any unknown defects with respect to the title to the property. Normally, the lender will require a title insurance policy as a condition of the loan.

Conclusion to Buying a Home

A real estate transaction can be complex and involves many parties and documents. When purchasing a home, you as the buyer should do your homework, be sure to read all documents involved in the transaction and seek professional advice in the event that you do not fully understand any aspect of your transaction.

In the event that you use the services of a real estate licensee and believe he/she mishandled your purchase transaction, you should file a complaint with the Bureau of Real Estate.

Chapter Source

State of California - Department of Consumer Affairs - Bureau of Real Estate, Information for Homebuyers

6.

SELLING YOUR HOME

As they say, you only get one chance to make a first impression and the same can be said for your home. If you're putting your house on the market, it's important that you take the necessary steps to ready it for potential homebuyers and ensure that it stands out from the rest. In Playa Vista where condominium complexes dominate you may be competing against the exact same floor plan in the exact same building. You're also in competition with similar sized units that may be in a different complex. The point is, competition can be stiff and if you're eager to get your house sold, you need to make it stand out and shine!

When selling a detached home outside of a planned community, the work starts outside the home with gardens, lawns and other landscaping. The great thing about Playa Vista is that all of that work is taken care of through the HOAs for the community and for your building. Everything is always in ship shape.

So the questions are, where do you start and what do you do to maximize your return on your investment and get your house sold.

If you've selected a knowledgeable, local real estate agent to list your property, we can assume that they've done the necessary research and comparisons to get your house priced right to attract buyers and hopefully get some offer activity. The following is what you can do in order to showcase your home. Potential buyers should be wowed when they come through the door and if they've seen a similar unit elsewhere in the area, you want yours to make them forget about all of the others.

As I mentioned, the curb appeal of your home has been taken care of, but what can you do to improve the first impression before somebody even enters your condominium? You can start with your doorway. Make sure the door is clean and free of scuff marks, dust or other dirt particles. You probably can't repaint your door without HOA approval and the properly colored and type of paint, but some hot soapy water and elbow grease will work just fine. You can also add a nice plant if you have room for it and a clean welcome mat. Finally make sure the outside lights are working and the sconces are clean as well.

In most cases you're still going to be living in your home while you're trying to sell it. This can present challenges, but you'll need to do a little extra work to de-clutter and keep things tidy during this time. You should start by removing the personal items like photographs or even artwork that may not be appealing to everyone. You'll want to create a clean slate so potential buyers can see past your stuff and envision their own things in the home.

Vacate the home
When your house is being shown to buyers, you'll generally be given fair warning of their arrival or you've scheduled an open house in advance so you can plan your time accordingly. It's important that you're not home during this time so they can feel comfortable during the showing and can speak freely with the agent about their thoughts, concerns or desire to place an offer. It's probably best if you leave before anyone arrives so they don't see that you've only departed for their benefit since they may feel rushed.

Kids and pets
Kids and pets may be cute, but they shouldn't be part of the sales process. If you're kids are old enough to be home alone, make sure that they're aware of the sales process and what they need to do if somebody is coming to view your home when you're not there.

Scale down the contents

In the chapter on preparing for your move we also talk about getting rid of things you might not need or use anymore. The best time to start this process is when you've listed your home and you're preparing it for viewing. If you're not in a big rush, you may be able to hold your yard sale or start selling some items. If you don't have the time available, this might be the time to rent a storage unit and move out extra "stuff". In some cases this may be extra chairs, side tables, or that exercise machine in the spare bedroom.

Although we live in California and the weather stays pretty nice year round, you might have certain collections of clothes that you only wear during certain seasons. People love walk-in closets, but you don't want it so crammed with stuff that it looks too full. See if you can gather up enough clothes to send to temporary storage to make it look tidy and open. If you want to go the distance you could arrange clothes in order by type and color.

Book shelves can look cluttered no matter how hard you try to make it look tidy and organized. Clear off the majority of the book shelves and if it's not a built in unit, it might be a good idea to put it into storage as well. For built in units you can display a few nice books or place non-personal items with some accent lighting.

If you have young children with a lot of toys, you'll need to tidy up when they're done playing and put the toys into a storage bin or area to keep them out of sight. If you're able to sneak some larger things away from them for a couple months, you might choose to send some to storage as well.

Small appliances can really fill a kitchen in a hurry and cause the clutter look to occur once again. Move out the toaster oven, waffle maker and any other items that you won't be using for a while.

Now that the house is free of unnecessary furnishings, clothing, appliances and the like, it's a good time to give it a once over and a deep cleaning.

Depending on your home and whether you have kids and pets, it may require professionals. New owners may tear up the carpet or replace other things, but steam cleaning and hiring a professional maid service might be a solid investment that will help get it sold quickly. Give the bathrooms full attention and make sure mildew and mold is removed and water spots on fixtures and glass are gone as well.

Preparing for showings
When preparing to open the doors to potential buyers you want to make the best impression possible. This means, taking care of all those little details that make the other person feel at ease so they fall in love with your house.

Entice their sense of smell. While scented candles are nice, they often give off fumes that can aggravate sensitive sinuses, not to mention stain the walls. A better solution would be to use a lightly-scented potpourri, plug in oil warmers or cinnamon sticks. Don't go overboard and don't combine several different scents or you might end up chasing potential buyers out if it gets too overpowering.

Eliminate unpleasant odor sources. Limit pets and their litter boxes from the main areas of your home during viewings. Open the windows whenever possible to air out places where odors could reside. Don't go overboard with odor-masking sprays, as this can backfire and call attention to the odor rather than eliminating it.

Add music to their ears. Light, relaxing mood music played at a low volume can enhance your potential buyer's perception of your property. Place a radio in each room so that those viewing your house will hear soothing sounds as they move throughout. Make sure to play it quietly on a soft jazz station so that it is only an accent, and not a distraction when buyers tour each room.

If your agent isn't able to assist with staging your home you might consider hiring somebody that's trained to do so. These are specialists with interior design skills who come in and actually rearrange your furniture. They design your home to make it more appealing to buyers. Although real estate professionals are more than capable of giving you insider secrets to sell your home for top dollar—and some even have interior design skills themselves— they also have access to professional stagers who can give your property an additional edge.

In a competitive market where buyers are calling the shots, a professional stager can help you present a polished home to attract multiple offers. Speak with your real estate professional and ask them to help you determine if hiring a professional stager makes sense within your budget. If it looks like you can make the money for hiring a stager back through a better sale price and gain a substantial profit from it, then it is definitely worth the money spent. This is especially true if you have a luxury home, where buyers will expect a high-end appearance. If luxury buyers are the demographic that will be viewing your property, you need to remember that their tastes are a great deal more discriminating. So you need every competitive edge you can get.

Chances are that, each buyer who comes through your front door is looking at multiple properties. You need to clearly and accurately set your property apart from the competition. By the end of the day, that buyer might not even remember which property had the features they really liked the best. That's why you should consider creating a brief, informational sheet that calls out all the special features within your home.

Here is where your agent's expertise really pays off. Agents are with buyers all day, every day. They know exactly what most buyers have on their wish lists, and they know what features you should call out and list toward the top of your one-page flier. Keep in mind that you don't want to list everything. What one person sees as an appealing feature, another might consider a detriment. Ask your agent to help you list just the best features to showcase.

First and foremost, listen to your real estate professional. Not only do they have the expertise you need to maximize your home's positive attributes, they are also a valuable source for that much-needed reality check. Your agent is with buyers every day. They know who is buying and what they are looking for. They can tell you what features your home has that will be highly desirable in today's market. The upgrades that you've made might be appealing to you, but your agent will know if they'll appeal to a potential buyer.

Make your feature sheet short and concise. A buyer will not care if you spent thousands of dollars to put in the new tiles in the bathroom. They will only care that the tiles are new and a color they like. Keep in mind, those tiles might not be that buyer's taste. They may actually want to rip it out if they buy the house.

List all new fixtures and functional items. If you just put a new roof on the house, installed a new water heater, updated the central air system or added new plumbing, these are things to draw attention to. New fixtures mean that the buyer won't have to worry about them breaking down any time soon. That's very appealing.

Don't get too attached to your decorative upgrades. These are all a matter of taste. You can list some small details— such as crown molding, new rugs and hardwood floors—but keep in mind that a home's beauty is still very much a matter of personal taste.

If you are leaving the refrigerator and the washer and dryer with the house, mention that. All of these things are a plus to a new home buyer who might not already own them. These are one less thing they have to worry about buying if they decide to purchase your house versus another that might not come with such amenities.

Everyone loves color. The problem is, everyone loves different KINDS of color. Therefore, when preparing your home to sell, you need to adjust your home's color scheme to a more neutral palette. The goal is to make it easy for the buyer to see their own belongings within your home. If you have bright walls and all of their furniture is understated, they are not going to see your home as a match for them. It just won't meet their style. Seeing a neutral color on the walls provides that buyer with the blank slate they need to imagine their own possessions within your home. It allows them the opportunity to form that important attachment.

Walk through your home and take inventory of all the walls that are painted and what color they are. Ultimately, you want to paint each room a light tan or off white, but first you need to prioritize. The first room your potential buyer will see is the first you should adjust, and the one you should pay a great deal of attention to. A can of primer and some neutral-colored paint will go a long way toward making that room look like it could accommodate any decorative style the buyer might prefer. One bit of additional advice is to use masking tape for edges and at the ceiling. If you're not a pro, no matter how steady or how great you are at painting than everyone else, you probably aren't steady enough. Painting badly may be worse than not painting at all.

Consider Removing all wallpaper. Wallpaper is a huge roadblock to new buyers because it has your personal style stamped all over it. If you're experienced in doing this kind of thing yourself, go for it. If not, hire a professional. You don't want to maul a room in the process of trying to improve it. The small amount of money you put into hiring a professional to remove your wall paper, sand down the area and paint it a neutral tone will be returned to you in the end when you sell. You are only going to get top dollar for a home that is in top selling form.

Pay special attention to smaller rooms, as color and presentation there are very important. If you've painted your small, second bedroom a deep red, this will actually make it look cramped. Dark colors tend to close in a space. A light, neutral color will actually open up the room and make it appear larger than it really is.

Even though today's home seller has access to more information than sellers in the past, you should still think twice when selling your home without the help of a real estate professional. Placing a home on the market is a full-time job that requires the experience, time and expertise to help make the most of that sale. According to the National Association of Realtors,® two-thirds of people who have sold their homes themselves say they would not do so again.

Why? Money.

Simply put, having a Realtor® could get you more money in the long run, even when it means handing over a small portion of the sale. Real estate professionals know what home buyers are looking for and can help your home stand out, especially in a cooling market.

Let your home shine. Getting more money for your property isn't just about knowing the market and advertising your home. It's about knowing what will make your home stand out and helping it outshine the competition. This is especially true when selling a home in a buyer's market. Every additional edge helps, and your agent can help you display your home at its best.

Realtors® know exactly what home buyers are looking for in today's market. They have a good handle on what your home can sell for and what buyers really want in a home. Remember, they are out there dealing with the market every day. They know who's buying and what entices them into making an offer. Before placing your home on the market, most agents will walk through it with you to get a feel for any adjustments that need to be made so that your home is showcased to inspire offers. This kind of insight is invaluable, and will get you more money for your home in the end.

A real estate agent provides a buffer between the seller and the buyer. Selling your home is an emotional time. It isn't necessarily a time you want to be haggling over the value of your house and all the memories you have wrapped up in it. In most cases, it's good to have someone else do the tough negotiation for you. Without their assistance, you are much like a ship at sea without an anchor. There is nothing to stabilize you and provide that needed reality check when things get emotional. A Realtor® knows how to keep things moving forward in a productive way, and ultimately helps you make the most of your real estate investment.

Preparing your home for sale can be a daunting task, but with the help of your real estate professional and the insider secrets they have to share, it can be done quickly and easily. The most important thing to remember is that the better you display your property, the more money it will sell for. Let your agent help showcase your home so that it really stands out against the competition of today's market. Make the effort now, and you will soon reap the rewards when you cash in on your real estate investment.

8.

THE HOMES IN PLAYA VISTA, CA

Within Playa Vista, there are two phases that were constructed more than a decade apart. Due to the economic downturn and various delays as a result of environmental studies, the second phase only began construction in 2012.

The initial phase which began construction in 2001 includes single family, condominium and apartment homes while phase two includes a similar combination of brand new dwellings.

The following pages provide summaries of the single family homes and condominiums in each phase.

Phase 1 - Single Family

Icon

3-Story Detached Residences
3,200 - 3,700 Sq. Ft.
2 – 5 Bedrooms, 3.5 - 4 Baths
Up to 4-Car Private Garage

As one of Playa Vista's premier collections, Icon offers 62 luxury, single-family detached and paired residences clustered around a brand new park. With the look and feel designed for an urban-setting residence, Icon presents an attractive array of architectural designs ranging from Spanish to Transitional.

Mondrian

3-Story Detached Residences
Up to 2,800 Sq. Ft.
3 – 4 Bedrooms, 3.5 - 4 Baths
2-Car Private Garage

Following the success of their 51 homes at Capri Court and their 31 homes at Matisse, Lee Homes designed Mondrian. Mondrian is an artistic collection of 16 vibrant, contemporary, single-family homes located next to the tranquil Celedon Park and across from the picturesque bluffs.

Capri Court by Lee Homes

3-Story Detached Residences
Up to 2,800 Sq. Ft.
3 – 4 Bedrooms, 3.5 - 4 Baths
2-Car Private Garage

The upscale, single-family homes of Capri Court offer inventive interior floor plans on multiple levels. These architecturally distinctive homes, inspired by 1940s West LA architecture, offer a mix of Mediterranean styles clustered around beautifully landscaped motor courts.

Cielo By Lennar Homes - Year Built 2012

3-Story Detached Residences
3,200 to 3,900 Sq. Ft.
3 – 4 Bedrooms, Up to 4.5 Baths
2-Car Private Garage

These Cielo homes are three and four-bedroom detached homes with up to four and one-half bathrooms and two to three-car garages. Encompassing approximately 3,202 to 3,899 square feet of living space, these sprawling floor plans come with large kitchens and spacious great rooms, perfect for entertaining.

Matisse by Lee Homes

3-Story Detached Residences
2,100 to 2,700 Sq. Ft.
2 – 4 Bedrooms, 3.5 Baths
2-Car Private Garage

Possibilities and the promise of an exceptional lifestyle await at Matisse, Lee Homes community of 31 detached homes at Playa Vista. These multi-level, single-family homes include terraces, media rooms, exercise rooms, home offices, and spectacular master suites.

Park Houses

3-Story Detached Residences
~ 3,500 Sq. Ft.
3 – 4 Bedrooms, Up to 4.5 Baths
2-Car Private Garage

These distinctive, contemporary, detached homes are designed with three living levels created for an elegant urban lifestyle. Two different, imaginative floor plans offer approximately 3,500 square feet of living space, including a minimum of three bedrooms.

Phase 1 - Condominium

Avalon

1 or 2- Story Homes
1-2 Bedrooms and 2 plus Den

Avalon sits in great location in Playa Vista on Pacific Promenade between Seawalk Drive and Kiyot Way. All the amenities of the CenterPointe Club, including the gym and pool are just steps away from the Avalon residence. Concert Park and the Shops at Concert Park are also just a block away.

Bridgeway Mills Townhomes
5300-5400 Playa Vista Drive
Up to 3-Story Attached Residences
1,450 - 2,450 Sq. Ft.
2 Bedrooms, Up to 3.5 Baths
3-Car Private Garage

Bridgeway Mills is located in the Fountain Park District, adjacent to Ballona Creek. Its contemporary architecture boldly challenges the conventions of design and geometry to create a unique, open environment of soaring walls, precise angles and gentle curves.

Carabela

12975 Agustin Place
1 or 2-Story Homes
1,065 to 2,200 Sq. Ft.
1-2 Bedrooms and 2 plus Den
Up to 2.5 Baths

Situated around garden courtyards, the four story buildings convey old California elegance. Carabela offers five distinctive single-level and two-story condominium home designs offering approximately 1,065 to 2,200 square feet, with 2 to 3 bedrooms, up to 2.5 baths and two-car subterranean parking.

Catalina
12963 Runway Road
1 or 2-Story Homes
1,065 to 2,200 Sq. Ft.
1-2 Bedrooms and 2 plus Den
Up to 2.5 Baths

Catalina condominiums are available in both one and two-story configurations. The residences of Catalina feature a combination of two-bedroom and two-bedroom plus den floor plans oriented to look outward toward streets and walkways, maximizing privacy of residents.

Chatelaine
5721 S Crescent Park West
1 or 2-Story Homes
1,550 to 2,850 Sq. Ft.
2 Bedrooms and 2 plus Den
Up to 2.5 Baths

Chatelaine is one of Playa Vista's premiere buildings situated in Playa Vista's Crescent Park. Chatelaine provides a concierge, business center, club room, outdoor fireplace, park adjacent to building, and private pool and spa.

Concerto Lofts - 2007
13045 Pacific Promenade
1,135 to 1,435 Sq. Ft.
1 or 2 Bedrooms
Up to 2.5 Baths

If you long to live the ultimate urban lifestyle in a contemporary loft inspired home, you've come to the right place. Concerto Lofts is the new distinctive neighborhood with all of the best elements of loft living. With every important convenience located at your doorstep, you'll never have to leave home.

Coronado
7100 Playa Vista Drive
1 or 2-Story Homes
1,100 to 2,500 Sq. Ft.
1 to 2 Bedrooms and 2 plus Den

You work hard so why shouldn't your lifestyle be easy? These low maintenance one and two-story condominium homes enjoy an outstanding location within Playa Vista near the CenterPointe Club, walking trails and the Sports Park.

Crescent Walk
13200 Pacific Promenade
1 or 2-Story Homes
623 to 1,400 Sq. Ft.
1 to 2 Bedrooms and 2 plus Den

Crescent Walk offers contemporary-styled single-level condominiums and multi-level town homes for a broad range of residents, including young singles and couples just starting out, bi-coastal commuters and suburban professionals wanting a place in the city.

The Dorian - Built 2007
6241 Crescent Park West
1 or 2-Story Homes
1,636 to 2,865 Sq. Ft.
2 to 3 Bedrooms
2 to 3 Bathrooms

With all the elegance and concierge-style services you'd expect from such a prestigious address. Now imagine looking out your window at the Ballona Wetlands, the breathtaking bluffs beyond or Crescent Park. This is The Dorian, Playa Vista's most exclusive condominium building.

Esplanade
13080 Pacific Promenade
1 or 2-Story Homes
1,636 to 2,865 Sq. Ft.
1 to 2 Bedrooms Some with Dens
2 to 3 Bathrooms

Esplanade gathers a combination of town homes and single-level condominiums around romantic courtyards. A carriage-entry court and a central lobby serve as portals to a series of courtyards and walkways with Italianate detailing reminiscent of seaside Mediterranean villas.

The Lofts

13020 Pacific Promenade
1,000 to 1,500 Sq. Ft.
1 to 3 Bedrooms
2 to 3 Bathrooms

One of the most intriguing housing opportunities at Playa Vista is The Lofts near Concert Park. The ceilings are high, the walls almost non-existent, the interior space is avant-garde contemporary and the architecture is South of France romantic.

The Metro

5625 Crescent Park West

1 or 2-Story Homes
1,230 to 2,160 Sq. Ft.
2 Bedrooms Some with Dens
2 to 3 Bathrooms

The striking Art Deco-style architecture of the Metro is considered to be a monumental focal point of Playa Vista's upscale Crescent Park District. These residences are a tribute to the heritage of Southern California architecture of the 1930s and 1940s. Dramatic facades frame the elliptical end of Crescent Park.

Paraiso
13173 Pacific Promenade
1 or 2-Story Homes
1,703 to 2,879 Sq. Ft.
2 to 3 Bedrooms Some with Dens
2 to 3 Bathrooms

Paraiso, Portuguese for "paradise", offers an ingenious mix of two-story town homes that are luxurious in both design and quality. Situated on Playa Vista Drive, directly North from The Center Pointe Club, the residences of Paraiso are created in two distinctive architectural styles.

Primera Terra
12920 Runway Road
1-Story Homes
965 to 1,504 Sq. Ft.
2 to 3 Bedrooms
2 Bathrooms

Located at the eastern-most portion of Phase I in the Playa Vista master planned community, this neighborhood organizes homes around a central courtyard that provides intimate 'outdoor rooms' for residents to relax and reflect.

Promenade
13044 Pacific Promenade
1 or 2-Story Homes
916 to 1,819 Sq. Ft.
Bedrooms - 1, 2, 1+ Den & 2+ Den
2 to 3 Bathrooms

The Promenade includes a mix of single-level and two-story condominium residences created in a contemporary style. Floor plans include one bedroom, one bedroom plus den, two bedrooms, two bedrooms plus office area and two bedroom plus loft designs.

Serenade

13031 Villosa Place

1 or 2-Story Homes

1,560 to 2,830 Sq. Ft.

2-3 Bedrooms

2.5 to 3 Bathrooms

Elegant town homes reminiscent of classic craftsman architecture offered in an ingenious mix of two-story town homes that are luxurious in both design and quality. Conveniently located near Concert Park and "Bark Park", all homes surround dramatic interior courtyards.

Tapestry
Multiple Streets
3 or 4-Level Homes
1,500 to 3,207 Sq. Ft.
2-4 Bedrooms
2.5 to 4 Bathrooms

Tapestry at Playa Vista represents urban living at its finest. Five, distinctive three- and four-level town home designs of Tapestry were created by The Steinberg Group, a noted, Santa Monica-based architecture firm. Tapestry offers gorgeous traditional architecture with attached 2 car garages.

Tempo
6020 Sea Bluff Drive
1 or 2-Story Homes
790 to 1,732 Sq. Ft.
1-3 Bedrooms
1 to 3 Bathrooms

Built by Standard Pacific Homes, Tempo's collection of 116 urban flats and two-story condominiums are set above street-level retail in the dynamic Concert Park district. Tempo's five inviting designs have up to three bedrooms and 2.5 baths in 932 to 1,732 square feet of living space.

Villa d'Este
5935 Playa Vista Dr
1 or 2-Story Homes
1,260 to 2,143 Sq. Ft.
2 to 3 Bedrooms
2 to 3 Bathrooms

Inspired by LA's Spanish Colonial revival mansions of the 1920s, Villa d'Este offers homes with the characteristics of a small boutique hotel in Spain. Villa d'Este is designed to resemble three individual period mansions that were converted into two-story town homes and condominiums.

Villa Savona
7101 Playa Vista Drive
2-Story Homes
1,180 to 1,680 Sq. Ft.
2 Bedrooms
2 to 2.5 Bathrooms

Inspired by Italianate Villas, Villa Savona homes offer the characteristics of a small European boutique hotel. Villa Savona is designed to resemble three individual period mansions that were converted into two-story town homes and condominiums.

Waterstone

6400 Crescent Park East

1-Story Homes
770 to 1,265 Sq. Ft.
1 to 2 Bedrooms
1 to 2 Bathrooms

Fresh and innovative, Waterstone presents a diverse collection of easy-living flats and condominiums located within the Crescent Park district of Playa Vista. An eclectic selection of eight distinctive designs range from 770 to 1265 square feet with 1 and 2 bedrooms and 1 to 2 baths.

Phase 2 - Single Family

Woodson by TRI Pointe Homes

3-Story Detached Residences
2,119 - 2,318 Sq. Ft.
3 – 5 Bedrooms, 3 ½ - 4 Baths
2-Car Private Garage and 1 Guest Space
Introduced in 2014 from $1,250,000 - $1,590,000

These tri-level single-family detached residences offer spaciousness ranging from approximately 2,119 to 2,318 square feet, including 3 to 5 bedrooms, 3.5 to 4 baths and a 2-car private garage plus one guest space. There's even a first-floor flex space that may be finished as an extra bedroom, a playroom, a game room, a hobby room or just about anything else you can think of. The Playa Vista lifestyle surrounds you with nearly everything you can imagine...shopping, dining, workout facilities, pools, parks, entertainment, live events, a new elementary school and a whole lot more...all within walking or biking distance of your doorstep.

Asher by KB Homes

3-Story Detached Residences
Approx. 2,435 – 2,757 Sq. Ft.
2 + Rec. Room – 5 Bedrooms, 2 Full + 2 Half – 4 Full + 2 Half Baths
2-Car Private Garage and 1 Guest Space
Introduced in 2014 from the Mid $1,000,000s

Each of Asher's three residence options, all three stories, include a private, built-in elevator, range in size from 2,435 to 2,757 square feet, and can include up to five bedrooms, four baths and they each have two-car garages. The community's emphasis on outdoor living is reflected in the multiple patio and deck spaces located on every floor of the homes. Asher at Playa Vista was honored in 2014 at the Pacific Coast Builders Conference (PCBC) with a Gold Nugget Award in the single-family detached home category.

The community's distinctive, angled floor plans maximize the living space within the homes by offering a fresh take on the "great room" concept favored by today's homebuyers.

Trevion by Brookfield Residential

2- and 3-Story Detached Residences
Approx. 3,020 – 3,949 Sq. Ft.
4 – 5 Bedrooms, 4 ½ – 5 ½ Baths
2-Car Private Garage and 1 Guest Space
Introduced in 2014 from $1,700,000 - $1,999,000

Trevion at Playa Vista limited collection of 22 spacious single-family detached residences blends city sophistication with laid back coastal living. Doing away with boundaries and creating the ultimate invitation – Trevion introduces a new order of indulgent indoor and outdoor living to Playa Vista, adding space, light and exhilaration. There's room to transform your environment – from a downstairs guest suite to a music room or home office, with lounges and lofts for relaxing or creative pursuits, abundant bedrooms for growing families and outdoor spaces large enough for entertaining or just playing around.

Spa-inspired master suites are set apart for privacy with walk-out decks for enjoying night skies or your morning coffee. Heightening your senses with the finest interior designs and finishes, you can finally have exactly what you've always wanted at Trevion.

Phase 2 - Condominium

Camden by Brookfield Residential

Single-Story Attached Residences
Approx. 1,601 – 2,192 Sq. Ft.
3 – 4 Bedrooms, 2 – 3 ½ Baths
2-Car Private Garage
Introduced in 2014 from $950,000 - $1,270,000

Camden in Los Angeles introduces a fresh type of attached living to the Playa Vista palette. It's where the East Coast brownstone blends with a beachy West Coast vibe. Combining tradition with the freestyle spirit of abundant windows, Camden's dramatic brick architecture makes an impressive statement. Three new single-level floor plan designs offer equal proportions high function and low maintenance. Imagine tons of natural light, smart open spaces and great decks as outdoor rooms. Stylish modern finishes with a bedroom count to satisfy a variety of lifestyles makes Camden so cool. One design offers a 4th bedroom space down a level…perhaps a creative office or private guest suite.

Skylar By KB Homes

Single-Story Attached Residences
Approx. 1,905 – 2,462 Sq. Ft.
3 + Den – 4 Bedrooms, 2 ½ – 3 ½ Baths
2-Car Private Garage
Introduced in 2014 from the Low $1,000,000s

The sleek designs at Skylar at Playa Vista offer the height of comfort and class, with great room living spaces, elegant kitchens, private garages, and EV charging stations. The three one- and two-story floor plans available at Skylar range between 1,905 and 2,449 square feet, with up to four bedrooms, three-and-a-half baths and two-car garages.

Each building is divided into 3 single-level homes that incorporate universal design and a semi-private elevator to provide an accessible path to any floor. The bottom floor unit that sits above the first floor private garages offers a flex space that can either be a family room, home office or a multi-generational suite for the flat above. Connected by way of a foyer and stair, the resident also has access to the home's main living floor by way of elevator. This flexibility of living arrangement truly provides a unique solution for buyers of any age, at any stage of life and can be used differently as the resident's needs change over time; allowing for a resident to gracefully age-in-place. Skylar is LEED Platinum Certification (with 95 points) maximizes market appeal, reduces expenses and optimizes health.

Fountainview - Los Angeles Jewish Home

Stylish Senior Living Independent-Living Residences
Approx. 840 – 2,300 Sq. Ft.
1 – 2 Bedrooms plus Den, 1 – 2 ½ Baths
Subterranean Valet Parking
Introduced in 2014 from the Mid $500,000s

In 2016, the Los Angeles Jewish Home will open Fountainview, a luxury senior living community, in beautiful Playa Vista. Designed with a host of desirable amenities and services to create a resort environment, Fountainview at Gonda Westside will blend comfort and elegance all the while fostering a sense of community and creating a legacy for the future. Residents will enjoy an active, independent lifestyle at Fountainview at Gonda Westside with a location that is just a short walk from restaurants, shops and other conveniences of Playa Vista.

9.

Area Statistics & Demographics

Median Home prices last four quarters

Q4/2013 ~$650,000
Q1/2014 ~$700,000
Q2/2014 ~$780,000
Q3/2014 ~$880,000

Median property taxes paid in 2011: ~$10,000

Total number of houses and condos 2013: 2,861

Total number of apartments: 1,375

For population 25 years and over:

High school or higher: 99.5%
Bachelor's degree or higher: 78.3%

Graduate or professional degree: 34.8%

For population 15 years and over in 90094:

Never married: 38.5%
Now married: 48.1%
Separated: 0.7%
Widowed: 0.5%
Divorced: 12.2%

Median resident age: 33.1

Average household size: 1.9

Median worker income: $73,945

Median family income: $147,604

Crime Level

The Crime Index compares the risk or probability of future occurrence of certain types of crime in this community as compared to the national average. The national average for each type of crime equals a score of 1.0, so a score of 2.0 would represent twice the risk as the national average, and a score of 0.50 would represent half the risk of the national average. The overall crime index for Playa Vista is 1.66*.

*Source: Onboard Informatics

Homes Sold per Quarter in 90094

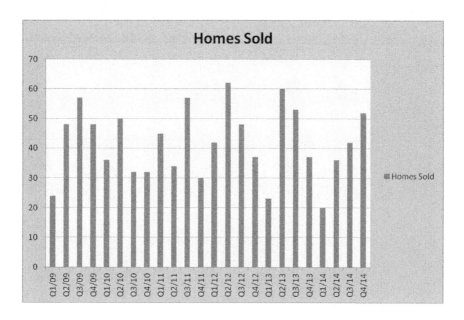

Homes Sold per Year in 90094

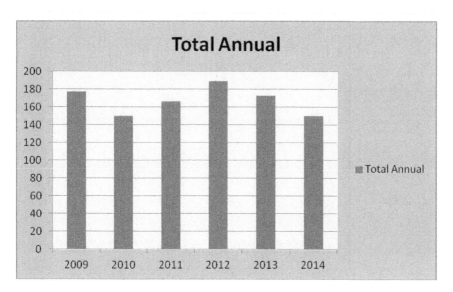

10.

Contact Tami Humphrey

I hope you've found value in this book and that you were able to learn a little more about the community that I call home. If you don't live here now, but you're thinking of doing so, I hope I can assist you in finding the perfect property. If you're already a resident and you're considering a move either to another area of Playa Vista or away from the community, I'd love to sit down to discuss the preparation and listing of your home.

I've been living and working here since 2006 and with my years of experience and knowledge of the various buildings that make up our community I feel confident that I can find exactly what you're looking to purchase or find a buyer that wants your home.

I want to make myself available to answer your questions about what you've read here or any other real estate questions you may have. You'll find details on how to contact me on the next page. I invite you to reach out anytime to ask your questions or to arrange a meeting.

Phone: (424) 228-8442

Email: info@PlayaVista-RealEstate.com

Website: www.PlayaVistaLiving.com

Made in the USA
Monee, IL
19 November 2021